Adopting Agathism

Georgia Alanis Campbell

BookLeaf Publishing

Presentation by *BookLeaf Publishing*

Web: www.bookleafpub.com

E-mail: info@bookleafpub.com

ISBN: 9789357618137

First edition 2022

For my mum

PREFACE

Agathism is a word that essentially means everything will be alright, there may be a rough road ahead but ultimately everything will be just fine. I think it's important to try and remind ourselves of this as much as possible and savour the small moments in life when we can just stop and take a deep breath.

Orange Leaves

Look out on
cool crisp mornings
Octobers brisk embrace.

Leaves crunch under
foot and paw,
early morning escape.

Stinging deep inhale,
sharp smell of
winter ever familiar.

Soon the trees
will be bare
from orange leaves.

Nostalgia beckons for
a year not
yet complete.

BST

Night's grasp
suffocating the day
already
we dream of summer.

Her time with us
not long spent
Sun kisses fade quickly
Summertime,
an echo on the wind.

Trick or Treat

Children dance
by front doors
eager impatience
counting the seconds
till sunset.
Head in hands,
leaning on the
windowsill
watching with eagle-eyed
stares.
Fidgeting in full costume.

"We need to wait till night-time!"

Stars start to
leak into view.
Empty bags greedily
wait to swallow all
the gifts on offer.
Gleeful laughter
consumes the night.

Winter '22

Safe haven, home.

Step inside,
cold air frosts
on every exhale
fingertips barely there

"Should I put the heating on? Or Maybe I just
need to eat?"

The ramifications
of either action
bounce around.
An unreasonable debate.

Another jumper and sleep,
that's free at least.

Presumptions

5

Look outside,
clear blue sky
bitter chill in the air.
Wrap up warm

Afternoon arrives
Sun beaming

Sweat beads forming

Remove a layer

Sweat still coming,
no more layers to remove,
Uncomfortable tension
as you navigate the day.

This outfit was a mistake.

Autumn Walks

Slip
Slide
Steady yourself

Find your footing.

Deep breath

another step

Gravity wins.

Ouch.

Cold ground
punching colder bones.

Mornings

The moon
still shines

stars stretch
across the sky

Ears peels
for footsteps
on the roof.

Excitement trembles,
itching to unwrap
what waits downstairs.

Morning seems
so far away

Surely it's morning?
It's dark enough.

Stairs squeaking
betray your intention.

Wait...

Light glowing
under closed doors.

He must be here!

Pick up the pace,
race downstairs,
eyes full of dreams.

Empty hands
already feel the
presence of presents.

"Go back to bed. It's been 10 minutes!"

Insomnia

Heavy rain
bashing the window
threatening to
shatter glass.

Toss
turn,
sleepless night
seems likely.

Violent brightness
of the phone
announces
morning is here.

If I go to sleep
right this second
I can get 4 hours.
Panic bubbles.

A full day of
work looms.
Alarms threatening
to scream at any second.

Daytime arrives,
the sun not
yet awake.
Cuddles from cold
air embrace you tightly.

Halloween

Sit down,
frothy hot chocolate
fuzzy blanket
fluffier socks

Knock at the door

Comfort disturbed
throw the throw

Another impatient knock

Door flung open
a sea of faces
gap tooth smiles
Trick or treat!

Tiny hands grasp
for everything
and anything
they can carry.

Scurry away
conversation
carries on the

cool night air.

You remember,
your favourite
night of the year.
Nostalgia sooths
the constant
inconvenience.

If i am
anything in life,
I will never be
the house that
gives you fruit.

Christmas Eve

Silence sweeps
while the city sleeps
snow threatens
to coat stray kittens.
A robin hops
commotion stops.
Christmas is here
a morning of tears
happy and sad
some fraught some glad.

Memories will be made
that eventually degrade
the love that binds them
forever a gem
something to cherish
when facts perish

Bittersweet

Counting down the seconds,
the bell rings,
three thirty sharp,
announcing freedom.

"That bell is for me not you."

Hangry groans ricochet.
Rush through corridors,
swept along by the tide.
Maybe today is the day.

"Please can we get a maccies?"
"No, we have food at home."

Get home.
Fear bubbles.
Shoes off.
Jacket thrown.

You spot,
a glimmer,
in the corner.
Dreaded red light.

The slow cooker is on.

Inbetween

15

Christmas day leftovers
burst out the fridge
boxing day buffet,
no dent was made.

Next year we really
should buy less.
A yearly chant
with no impact.

There are only
so many ways
you can reuse
no ones favourite food

How long will
it be before
turkey insanity
sets in?

Just a thought
of anything else
is tantalising
and torture.

In twelve months
we will have this
conversation over
and over.
An unspoken tradition.

Fear of new year swings round
Christmas still clings
we sit here,
food exhausted state.

Blink and it's gone.

Mental Welling

Nights sit heavy
suffocation
dark nights
dark days

Sunlight waves briefly

Too cold to move
Too irritable to rest
Constant
Confusion

"Have you tried taking a bath?"

If only I could
afford the hot water
Reminiscent scolding
Sensation

"Okay, what about a walk?"

I'm a woman.
Walking
alone
at night.

"It's not safe."

"You're not safe inside either."

Black Friday

A new TV, an obvious necessity.

People cannot eat
let alone find heat.

Yet here you stand,
queuing in the cold

for the top rated TV.

Following a day of thankfulness
feeling fortunate for what you have
the only better feeling
is to spend money on surplus things.

Material possessions
make for
material connections.
Deeply hollow
never satisfied.

There is always a new model.

2 meters

20

Guidelines trampled
by a thousand feet

A marker of respect
faded and worn

Distant memory
of social distancing.

Full Moon

She watches over me
Guiding me gently

How much she has seen
How much she much know

Wisdom with age
Beauty so raw

Her push and pull
changes us all.

1st January

22

New year
new promises

How long will
they last?

A year
of opportunity

A year
of disappointment

Which will it be?

Sunrise

Light mornings

Warmly welcome

Birds boast

Buds abound

Bountiful blossom.

Stand, wait

Sun soaked

Eyes closed

Deep breath

Fresh fragrance

Summers coming

Shifting Seasons

24

Spring flowers,
Aprils showers.
Parched earth,
Tree's rebirth.
Wicked wind,
Ewe's whined.
Freyja's prime,
Yearly paradigm.